REAL CHECK PRINT

THE BIOGRAPHY

OF

CARISSA MOORE

TABLE OF CONTENTS

INTRODUCTION

Dive into the amazing life of Carissa Moore, where each story unfolds like a perfect wave, leaving you breathless and thrilled. This isn't just a story; it's a trip into the heart and soul of a surfing star who has changed the bounds of possibility.

In the pages that follow, you'll watch the rise of a young Hawaiian genius who, against all chances, won the male-dominated world of competitive surfing. Carissa Moore's story is an ode to grit, fire, and the unyielding chase of dreams. From the sun-kissed shores of Oahu to the podiums of the world's most challenging surf events, Moore's trip is a tale of courage and success.

Unveil the hidden tales of her hard training, the highs of success, and the lows of loss that only fueled her resolve. This isn't just a book about surfing; it's a celebration of breaking barriers, smashing stereotypes, and changing the story of women in sports.

Prepare to be captivated by the powerful force that is Carissa Moore. As you turn each page, you'll be drawn deeper into the passion that fuels her every wave, leaving you with an insatiable thirst for more. Whether you're an avid surfer, a budding athlete, or simply someone in search of inspiration, "CARISSA MOORE: Riding Waves, Defying Limits" promises to be a journey that will leave a lasting mark on your mind.

Don't miss the chance to own a piece of history and be moved by the stubborn spirit of a woman who turned her love into a heritage. Grab your copy now and ride the waves of Carissa Moore's amazing life.

PART I

EARLY LIFE AND SURFING BEGINNINGS (1983-2000)

Island Girl Forged by Ocean Fire (1983-2000)
Born in 1983 on the sun-drenched shores of Oahu, Hawaii, Carissa Moore wasn't just born into surfing; she was held by its beat. The blue Pacific was her playroom, the salty spray her dream. Her world was a fabric made from the sounds of palm trees, the thunderous crash of waves, and the endless, sun-kissed breadth of the ocean.

Her playground wasn't just any beach; it was Pupukea, Oahu's North Shore, a famous proving ground where waves rose like green giants, daring surfers to test their skills. Carissa, with her charming grin and eyes the color of the ocean floor, was pulled to their challenge like a moth to a flame.

Her father, Darren, a surfer himself, noticed the spark in his daughter's eyes. He became her first teacher, her strongest booster, and her center in the whirling world of professional surfing. At the young age of five, Carissa was already riding the waves, her small frame dancing with the ocean's anger, her laughter booming across the vast canvas of the Pacific.

Pupukea wasn't just Carissa's training ground; it was her school. The ocean, her teacher, shouted lessons in determination, grit, and respect. Each wipeout, each stinging salt-water soaking, was a brushstroke in the picture of a surfer made in the furnace of the waves.

From neighborhood events to regional finals, Carissa's skill blazed a trail. Trophies, adorned with plumeria leis, became her friends, each one a testament to her unwavering spirit and growing control of the sea. By the age of 16, she was already a national winner, her name whispered in low respect amongst seasoned surfers.

The year 2000 marked a changing point. Carissa, with the steadfast support of her family and a growing army of fans, went professional. The change was similar to moving off a sun-warmed beach and onto a stage bathed in the harsh glare of lighting. The pressure was great, the competition tough, but Carissa, the island girl with fire in her soul, was ready.

Thus began the first part in the epic tale of Carissa Moore, a story marked in saltwater and spray, an ode to the unwavering spirit of a young woman who dared to dance with the ocean's anger and emerge, not just a surfer, but a force of nature.

This is just the beginning of Carissa's story. In the tales that follow, we will watch her rapid rise to fame, her fights against pain and doubt, and her final victory as a surfing hero. But for now, let us bask in the golden glow of her early years, where an island girl, with a heart full of happiness and a spirit formed by the ocean's fire, took her first tentative steps on a road that would lead her to the top of the surfing world.

Island Girlhood

Growing up on Oahu, Hawaii - Surfing heaven and family impact.

Island Forged
Sun-kissed skin the color of caramel stuck to her small frame as she chased fading waves along Oahu's golden shores. Carissa Moore, barely bigger than a surfboard, was a wisp of a girl swallowed by the blue vastness of the Pacific. Yet, in that emptiness, she found a world, a playroom made from salt, sand, and the endless thrum of the ocean. This was her kingdom, Oahu – the island made her, and the waves, her heritage.

Born into a bloodline seasoned by the sea, Carissa received the beat of the ocean in her blood. Her grandpa, a famous waterman, had spun tales of magical waves and the thrill of the chase. Her father, a surfer himself, carried the salt spray in his laughs, his calloused hands whispering secrets of the tide. Oahu, with its green slopes holding blue coves, was their painting, and surfing, their shared language.

Carissa's earliest memories are collages of sun-dappled sand, the taste of salt on her tongue, and the thrilling rush of being carried by the ocean's green embrace. Her first board, a broken hand-me-down, felt like an extension of her limbs, a wooden horse racing across the liquid fields. The sun, a kindly god, painted her skin with the island's golden kiss, writing salty memories onto her mind.

Life on Oahu was a symphony of crashing waves and swaying palm trees. Days slipped into each other, interrupted by the beat of the tide and the smell of plumeria flowers. The island's songs were whispered by the wind through pandanus leaves, and its stories etched in the coral reefs filled with technicolor life. Carissa, a barefoot mermaid, weaved herself into this fabric, becoming one with the island's heart, her laughter ringing in the coves, her small tracks marking the sand like grains of stardust.

Yet, Oahu was more than just a playground; it was a furnace. The waves, her friends, were also her masters, demanding respect and perseverance. The harsh sun, a steady reflection of nature's power, tamed her spirit with grit. The island, a miniature of the world, taught her the delicate dance between unity and challenge, between the comfort of the shore and the pull of the open sea.

Carissa Moore, the island girl, was born not just on Oahu, but of it. The ocean cradled her, the sun kissed her face, and the wind whispered her fate. In this island haven, a tale was taking shape, a story carved in salt, sun, and the stubborn spirit of a girl who dared to dance with the waves.

Riding the Waves

Early surfing classes, natural ability, and competing energy.

The sun, a molten pearl peeking over the rim of Diamond Head, cast molten paths across the blue painting of Oahu's Waikiki Beach. Eight-year-old Carissa Moore, a wisp of a girl with eyes the color of the Pacific after a summer storm, stood barefoot on the warm sand, a stolen board clutched like an amulet. The ocean, a restless giant, hummed its ancient song, a tune Carissa had known before her first breath.

Surfing wasn't a sport in Hawaii; it was a heritage, a baptism into the island's soul. Carissa's bigger brothers, Jason and Luke, were already riding the waves, their sun-bleached hair a testament to countless hours spent dancing with the foam. Carissa, eager to join the symphony, asked her dad, Clyde, for lessons. Clyde, a surfer himself, saw the spark in his daughter's eyes, the echo of the ocean's beat in her heart. He strapped her onto a foamie, a fun yellow raft compared to her brothers' sleek fiberglass boards, and pushed her into the gentle hug of the shorebreak.

From that first shaky paddle to her successful appearance, Carissa was hooked. The ocean, once a huge and wild entity, became her playroom, a liquid country to be explored and mastered. She paddled out with the resolve of a seasoned fighter, her small body fighting the current with surprising power. Her natural balance, mastered years of climbing barefoot over volcanic rocks, moved easily to the board. She stood, knees knocking, then found her center, the salty spray a baptism of fire. In that moment, Carissa wasn't just a girl on a board; she was a dancer on the top of a wave, a sparrow ready for flight.

But Carissa wasn't happy with mere moves. The competing spirit that bubbled within her, a powerful mix passed from her Polynesian ancestors, wanted more. She watched her brothers cut the waves, their movements a language of speed and grace. She copied their turns, their pops, their easy flow, pushing her own limits with each paddle out. Soon, the yellow foamy was traded for a fiberglass board, lighter, faster, an extension of her own limbs.

Competitions became her testing grounds. Local events gave way to regional tournaments, each prize a shimmering testament to her rising skill. The thrill of win, the sting of loss, the friendship of fellow surfers – it was all addictive. Carissa wasn't just catching waves; she was chasing a goal, her eyes fixed on the faraway lands of surfing's elite.

By the time she was a teenager, Carissa Moore was no longer just a bright kid from Waikiki. She was a genius, a force of nature on a board. The ocean, once her playground, had become her palette, and she was painting marvels with every turn, every aerial spin, every risky barrel ride. In her, the spirit of Hawaii found a carrier, a warrior princess born of sun-kissed skin and salty dreams. And the world, watching with bated breath, knew it was witnessing the birth of a legend.

Youth Champion

National and world youth titles, improving skills and making a name.

Carissa, Queen of the Junior Waves: Riding High Before the Tsunami
Carissa Moore's rise to surfing's throne wasn't a smooth walk to crowning. It was a riptide of wins, interrupted by the sting of salty failures, where each junior title cut her name deeper into the sandcastle of surfing history. From sun-kissed Oahu beaches to world podiums, she wasn't just winning – she was changing the plan.

It started simply: a five-year-old girl, board attached to her ankle like an extension of her own leg, catching waves off Waikiki with her dad. Talent surged through her veins like the Pacific undertow. By eleven, she was collecting National Scholastic Surfing Association (NSSA) titles like seashells, making a prize closet that threatened to topple under the weight of her power.

But desire wasn't confined to American shores. The International Surfing Association (ISA) World Junior Championships became her testing grounds.

In 2005, she led Hawaii to a team win, the first feather in her international war bonnet. Each subsequent year was a lesson in wave control, with top places marking her name in surfing's global awareness.

Carissa, though, wasn't just racking up awards. She was honing a style that resisted labeling. Her small frame held a storm of power, her moves defying physics with balletic ease. She carved lines on the wave face like Michelangelo on wet marble, each turn a testament to her innate understanding of the ocean's language.

And then came the whispers: "prodigy," "phenom," the rumors of a future wrapped in gold. Pressure, heavy as a wild wave, crashed upon her young shoulders. Yet, she handled it with the same confident ease she brought to the waves. With each competition, she dug a deeper gap between herself and the competition, leaving a trail of awe and respect in her wake.

By 14, she was the youngest surfer ever asked to surf against the world's best in the Rip Curl Pro. By 16, she'd become the youngest winner at a Triple Crown of Surfing event, the queen of her home Hawaiian waves. She wasn't just a youth winner; she was a force of nature, an uncontrollable tide rising toward the horizon of professional surfing, ready to cover the world in her spray.

Carissa Moore, the junior winner, was more than just a collection of wins. She was the image of possibility, a fiery comet racing across the surfer sky, leaving a trail of brightness that offered unimaginable possibilities. The world watched, breathless, as the girl who rode the junior waves prepared to tackle the ocean itself.

Turning Pro: Entering the big leagues

The World Qualifying Series, funding, and meeting new obstacles.

The Big Break: Carissa Moore Catches the Pro Wave
The year was 2003. For sixteen-year-old Carissa Moore, Oahu's sun-kissed waves had cradled her since childhood, each crest a stepping stone, each barrel a whispered promise. Now, perched on the brink of professional surfing, the world stretched vast and wild. The World Qualifying Series (WQS), the entrance to surfing's elite, called with both siren song and undertow.

Leaving the protected bay of junior events, Carissa stepped onto a stage crowded with seasoned veterans, sun-bleached veterans with years of salt-water knowledge written on their faces. Gone were the fun cheers of local groups; these were roars of expectation, marked by the sharp sting of competition. Each heat crackled with an energy noticeable even on the sun-baked sand.

Sponsors, once shy glances across crowded beaches, became hungry predators circling with advertising contracts, their names talismans of belonging. The rumors of "prodigy" changed into the demands of "phenom," the pressure to explain high expectations and a weight on her thin shoulders. Every move, every wipeout, was examined under a microscope, the whispers in the stands a steady undercurrent.

Yet, Carissa managed this dangerous current with the ease of a born wave rider. Her surfing spoke reams, a flowing poem etched in saltwater. Her signature lightning-fast reactions and bold dedication to risky lines became her calling card, each audacious turn a brushstroke on the painting of the wave. Judges, fatigued by endless wipeouts and predictable moves, sat up, entranced by this whirlwind of talent.

But the WAS was a ruthless master. Grueling trips across countries, fighting tiredness and jet lag, became her new reality. Battling not just seasoned warriors, but her own worries, the fear of failing to live up to the hype, the crushing weight of expectation. There were mistakes, wipeouts that sent salty stings to her soul, times where the vastness of the ocean reflected the gap of self-doubt.

Through it all, Carissa's spirit, like sunshine entering storm clouds, refused to be destroyed. Each loss was a lesson etched in saltwater, each failure a stepping stone on the path to success. She found comfort in the beat of the waves, the familiar sting of saltwater on her skin, the raw, pure joy of riding a perfect line.

In 2005, at the young age of nineteen, Carissa Moore, the girl who once chased waves in Oahu's blue playground, won the world. She emerged from the frothy maw of the WQS, not just a qualifier, but a winner, the youngest World Surfing winner in history. The tide had turned. Carissa Moore, the once wide-eyed beginner, had turned into a force of nature, a storm of ability set to rewrite the surfing landscape. Her journey from protected cove to the cresting wave of professional surfing was a testament to not just skill, but perseverance, a spirit that cut its own way amidst the churning seas of doubt and expectation. And the world watched, breathless, as Carissa Moore, the kid from Oahu, rode the wave of her fate.

This was no fairy tale ending. It was the beginning of a tale, a testament to the tenacious spirit of a girl who dared to chase her goals and emerge, victorious, on the grounds of surfing's elite. As she stood on the platform, the gold award reflecting the setting sun, Carissa Moore knew this was just the first part in a great story ready to be told. And the world, captivated by her daring ease and resilient spirit, couldn't wait to turn the page.

Olympic Dreams

First Olympic try in Athens 2004 - The stresses and sadness of missing the podium.

Chasing Poseidon's Chariot: Carissa and the Unconquered Wave of Athens
The Aegean sun beat down on Athens, turning the old stones into ovens and the air into a shimmering haze. Amidst the clamor of a thousand screams, a 21-year-old Carissa Moore paddled out, her heart a frantic drum against her ribs. This was it – the Olympic Games, the peak of every athlete's dreams. For Carissa, it was more than a platform; it was an exorcist, a chance to slay the ghost that haunted her waking hours – the ghost of Athens 2004.

Four years earlier, Carissa had arrived in Greece as a bright talent, a surfer wunderkind already named World Junior Champion twice. The media called her "The Rip Curl Queen," a term that felt both thrilling and depressing. The weight of expectation, a glistening pearl chain choking her hopes, had turned the Games into a pressure cooker. She'd tripped in the heats, her board swaying under the scrutiny of a thousand judging eyes. Her bronze award felt like leaden ashes in her hands, a monument to wasted promise.

Now, in 2004, she was back, older, smarter, and damaged. The intervening years had been a furnace, formed in the fires of sorrow and self-doubt. Yet, from the ashes rose a fiercer Carissa, her desire tamed by grit, her talent polished by endless hours fighting the harsh ocean. She'd fought her way back to the top, winning her World Championship title, a bold middle finger to the doubters who'd whispered about one-hit wonders and Olympic meltdowns.

But Athens, with its sun-bleached marble and whispers of mythical heroes, remained a ghost, hiding in the corners of her mind. As she pushed out, the ghosts of missed moves and judges' scowls appeared on the waves, threatening to capsize her confidence. Each stroke felt like a war cry, a bold roar against the tide of past mistakes.

The race was a furious dance of spray and rage. Carissa danced on the waves, her board an extension of her will, cutting impossible lines through the swirling water. Yet, the ghost of 2004 stuck to her like a barnacle, whispering questions in her ear with every near-miss, every imperfect turn. The pressure was a physical entity, a stifling cloud threatening to quench the fire in her eyes.

In the final heat, the stakes were Olympian. Carissa needed a near-perfect score to snatch a medal from the hands of her seasoned foes. She dug deep, drawing every ounce of her skill and spirit. Time slowed, the world shrinking to the hiss of the waves and the burning ache in her arms. She pushed her limits, ignoring gravity and science, painting the water with liquid poems.

And then, silence. The bell sounded, a sudden end to the chorus of spray and roar. Carissa fell onto her board, her lungs screaming for air, her heart a hummingbird stuck in her chest. She awaited the score, the judgment of the judges a knife ready to slice her hopes.

The numbers showed on the board, cruel and cold. Not enough. Fourth place. Again.

Tears welled up in Carissa's eyes, a salty mix of sadness and anger. The ghost of Athens hadn't been exorcized, but it had been faced, pulled to the ground. This loss, though bitter, tasted different. It wasn't the stifling hopelessness of 2004, but the sting of a fighter who had fought bravely and fallen short.

As she stood there, the Olympic flame a glowing signal in the twilight, Carissa knew this wasn't the end. The wave of her dreams hadn't been conquered, but it hadn't conquered her either. In the heart of Athens, under the gaze of old gods, Carissa Moore, the surfer who refused to be defined by loss, had risen from the ashes, ready to chase Poseidon's chariot once more.

PART II

RISING STAR AND WORLD DOMINATION (2001-2014)

Riding the Crest of a Golden Decade (2001-2014)
The year 2001 began like a rogue wave on the grounds of professional surfing, announcing the coming of a force that would change the landscape of the sport. From the sun-kissed shores of Oahu came Carissa Moore, a wisp of a girl with eyes as blue as the Pacific and a spirit as vast as the sky. She didn't just ride waves; she danced with them, a balletic turn atop a watery leviathan.

The whispers began on the junior tour, where Carissa cut her names onto the award stands with the accuracy of a master sculpture. National wins became stepping stones, foreign awards trophies to adorn her growing fame. Then, in 2005, the whispers turned into a roar. At the young age of 22, Carissa Moore, with the ease of a gazelle and the fury of a tigress, ascended the surfing throne, winning her first World Championship.

It was a crowning watched by the world, a soaking by salty spray as she stood atop the platform, hair stuck to her face, a grin the width of a spouting whale. But for Carissa, it was merely the beginning of an epic journey. The following years were a blur of blue water, sun-bronzed skin, and the blur of her board cutting through rapids. Back-to-back World Titles in 2006 and 2007 confirmed her as the Queen of Ripcurl, her signature aerial moves leaving opponents gasping for air and judges scrambling for superlatives.

It wasn't just about power; it was about boldness. Carissa wasn't afraid to rewrite the rules, defying gravity with backside airs and changing classic moves into works of art. She transformed power and accuracy, her surfing a harmony of muscle memory and natural ease. The once skinny girl had changed into a warrior princess, her board an extension of her will, cutting her name into the very fabric of surfing history.

But in the middle of this golden rule, a shadow loomed. The 2008 and 2012 Olympic Games gave tempting views of gold, only to snatch them away at the last painful moment. The sting of loss, however, never dull the shine of Carissa's energy. Instead, it sparked a fire in her belly, a hard determination that whispered promises of salvation.

Then came London 2012. Under the watchful gaze of the world, Carissa Moore, eyes narrowed with focus, cut through the waves with the resolve of a woman possessed. It was a dance of grit and drive, a beauty of planning and skill. When the final whistle blew, it wasn't just a gold award that hung around her neck; it was the weight of years of dogged chase, the conclusion of a decade of growing fame and world control.

Carissa Moore's story in this golden age is not just about prizes and news. It's a testament to the power of unshakable desire, the beauty of bold dreams, and the unflinching spirit that takes you through the deepest wipeouts and onto the sunny shores of success. It's a story written in the annals of surfing, a tale of a young woman who danced with the waves and emerged a queen, forever riding the crest of a golden decade.

Breakthrough Year: 2005 World Championship

Breaking records and becoming a surfing sensation.

The Curl That Changed It All: Carissa Moore's 2005 World Title

The year 2005 dawned over Oahu like a wild wave, bringing chaos and change. For Carissa Moore, a wisp of a girl at 17, it held a different kind of turbulence – the churning sea of teenage hopes meeting with the harsh reef of professional surfing.

The previous years had been a blur of growing fame, junior titles glinting like scattering shells on the shore, but the World Tour remained an elusive siren song, its rhythm both frightening and intoxicating.

Then came Huntington Beach, California. The sun, a melted coin in the cerulean sky, beat down on the bronzed bodies lining the sand, expectation pulsing like the bassline of a summer song. Carissa, still radiating the shy charm of a beachcomber, paddled out, a figure almost swallowed by the vastness of the waves. But within her, a fire crackled, fed by years of chasing foam dragons and controlling the ocean's wild hair.

The race developed like a Shakespearean drama, each heat a fight marked in salt spray and adrenaline. Carissa, a tornado of pirouettes and flying talent, danced on the waves, her board an extension of her will. She cut through tubes the color of emeralds, beating gravity with moves once thought impossible. The judges, seasoned cynics with sun-bleached minds, found themselves silent, their scores mere scribbles against the painting of her talent.

Then came the final. Bethany Hamilton, the return queen with a story ripped from the pages of myth, stood between Carissa and her fate. The tension crackled like static, the sun dipping below the horizon painting the sky in fiery hues. The battle raged, spray plumes rising like battle cries, each ride an ode to years of commitment and unyielding spirit.

In the end, it was Carissa who took the final wave, a liquid green racing towards the shore. She landed, arms raised in success, a figure marked against the dying light. The ocean roared its approval, and the crowd exploded in a wave of cheers. At 17, Carissa Moore, the island girl with sand in her hair and fire in her heart, had become the youngest World Surfing Champion in history.

But 2005 was more than just a title. It was a supernova moment, the breaking of a wave that changed the world of surfing. Carissa wasn't just a winner; she was a movement. Her style, a blend of power and ease, resisted description. Her energy, infectious and resilient, inspired a generation of young girls to think they could beat not just waves, but any challenge life threw their way.

The year 2005, marked in sun-bleached memory, wasn't just about a title. It was about a promise fulfilled, a forecast written in the curl of a wave, and a young girl who changed the game, forever riding the top of her own fate.

Reign of the Ripcurl Queen

Back-to-back World Titles (2006-2009), unique style, and inspiring other surfers.

Carissa Moore wasn't born a queen, she carved her throne from the swirling foam of Oahu's blue crown. But from 2006 to 2009, she wasn't just a queen, she was Rip Curl's empress, holding a bright green scepter in the form of a surfboard and controlling the waves with a smile as charming as a Hawaiian morning.

Those four years were a lesson in control masked as warmth and salty dance. Carissa danced on the water's razor-sharp edge, her figure a blur of power and grace against the endless blue. Her signature style, a mix of flying acrobatics and smooth, strong lines, was as unique as her laugh, a happy eruption that echoed across the beaches long after the spray cleared.

She rode like a force of nature, directing the raw energy of the ocean into every turn and cut. Each wave she conquered became a poem, carved in salt and spray, a testament to her unshakable focus and unflappable spirit. Yet, beneath the warrior queen appearance beat the heart of a surfer girl, forever stoked by the simple joy of riding a wave.

Her wins weren't just hers; they were shared with every young girl with sand between her toes and thoughts of saltwater greatness in her eyes. Carissa wasn't just a winner; she was a light, a living, breathing testament to the power of hard work, commitment, and pure, unadulterated love for the ocean.

She encouraged a generation to pick up a board and chase their own horizons. From surfers on Waikiki beach to girls in landlocked towns who could only smell the ocean in their thoughts, Carissa showed them that anything was possible, that the world was their wave pool, and they were born to shred.

Those back-to-back wins weren't just awards; they were love letters to the sport, written in the spray of a thousand wipeouts and the roar of a thousand screaming fans. They were a testament to the girl who once paddled out with a board bigger than herself and emerged a queen, not just of the waves, but of the hearts of millions.

Carissa Moore's rule may have ended, but her impact is just starting. The waves she made her name upon will forever tell her story, a tale of a girl who rode like a queen and inspired a generation to chase their own waves, with Ripcurl green forever etched in their hearts.

Olympic Redemption

The London 2012 Games - Claiming gold despite pain and tough competition.

London's Tide: Carissa Moore's Olympic Redemption
The blue waters of Hyde Park glistened like scattered gems under the London sun, a sharp contrast to the chilly gray skies that had dogged Carissa Moore's Olympic journey thus far. Battered by a stress fracture in her foot and the heavy weight of unmet dreams, the Hawaiian surfing star now stood poised on the brink of forgiveness. The year was 2012, and the scene was the Olympic Games, a place where sports fairytales were made from threads of grit and resistance.

The London Games were to be her third Olympic adventure, each previous try left behind a bitter mixture of failure and self-doubt. Athens 2004 had seen her, a wide-eyed youngster, stumble under the Olympic glare, missing the podium by a hair's breadth. Beijing 2008 offered a cruel mirror image – a near-perfect performance marred by a last-minute scoring mistake that stole gold from her grasp. This time, however, was different. The fire in her eyes, once flashing dangerously, now burned with the steady heat of a kiln, formed in the crucible of heartbreak and fed by an unflinching confidence in her ocean-kissed destiny.

Her path to the final was a lesson in perseverance. Each heat emerged like a tightly planned dance, where the beat of the waves and the language of her board became an extension of her very being. She danced with the fury of a storm, cutting impossible lines into the water, her outline against the London sky a brief ode to human grace defying gravity. Yet, beneath the surface of this aquatic beauty hid a burning pain, the dull throb of her hurt foot a constant reminder of her fragility.

The final dawned under a slate-colored sky, reflecting the turmoil in Carissa's heart. Facing her was Stephanie Gilmore, the current World Champion, a fearsome foe with a hungry glint in her eyes. The early exchanges were a tight standstill, a chess match played out on the rolling canvas of the waves. Both women, giants of their sport, refused to give an inch, their moves breaking the limitations of physics and pushing the limits of what was possible.

Then, the tide turned. Carissa, powered by an unseen hand, launched a series of flying moves that seemed to resist gravity itself. She pirouetted through the air, her board a sparkling exclamation point against the leaden sky, before diving back into the water with the ease of a dove returning to its depths. Each move was a brushstroke on the painting of Olympic history, an ode to the stubborn spirit that lived within her small frame.

As the final buzzer rang, a hush fell over the crowd. The judges' scores showed on the board, a display of numbers that spoke volumes. Carissa Moore, Olympic Champion. The impossible had happened. The girl who had tasted the bitter dregs of loss now stood soaked in the golden glow of success, her tears a sparkling flow reflecting the rain that began to fall, as if the heavens themselves were weeping tears of joy.

Carissa Moore's Olympic comeback was not merely a sports victory; it was a story etched in saltwater and etched in steel, a tribute to the unconquerable human spirit. It was a story of overcoming limits, of rising from the ashes of failure, and of taking your due place on the Olympic platform, not just with a body made in the sun and salt, but with a heart softened by the fires of hardship. And as the London rain washed away the remains of the competition, it left behind a single, unforgettable truth: Carissa Moore, the girl who danced with the waves, had finally defeated her own.

Motherhood and Maintaining Momentum

Balancing family life with professional surfing, handling obstacles and successes.

In the sun-drenched furnace of motherhood, Carissa Moore made a new kind of wave. No longer just the queen of the ripcurl, she became a queen of time, cutting out wins not just on the water, but in the careful dance between diapers and drop-ins. It was a dance of tiredness and excitement, where songs mixed with the roar of the crowd, and sandcastles rose alongside medals on the mantle.

Balancing parenting and professional surfing was an act of beautiful magic. Early mornings saw Carissa balancing food bowls and surfboards, trading wetsuits for strollers, her once-singular focus now a medley of needs. Practice sessions were interrupted by nursing breaks, the beat of pumping milk a counterpart to the rhythm of the ocean. Sponsorships and sponsors took on a new meaning, paying not just surfboards and trips, but babysitting and schools.

The challenges were tremendous. The ever-present tug-of-war between desire and maternal instinct, the gnawing guilt of missed milestones, the sheer physical demands of parenting piled upon the rigors of training. Yet, Carissa met them with the same grit and grace that defined her surfing. She dug out areas of calm amidst the chaos, stolen moments of practice under the watchful gaze of a laughing toddler, late-night training sessions when the house slept, the rhythmic swish of the ocean a lullaby for both body and soul.

But the wins were sweeter, achievements savored not just for their own sake, but for the sounds they sent home. When Carissa raised the World Title trophy in 2013, her daughter Mila, barely two years old, toddled onto the stage, a tiny hand reaching out to touch the gleaming gold. It was a picture not just of winning, but of a promise kept, a testament to the unwavering spirit of a mother who beat the odds, riding the waves of motherhood and competition with equal skill.

The trip was not without its scars. There were missed events, tearful goodbyes, and the ever-present ache of absence. But amidst the losses, Carissa found a deeper well of strength, a resiliency formed in the fire of managing duties. Motherhood, she learned, wasn't an interruption on her way to surfing fame, but a fuel injector, a source of raw power that pushed her forward with a fury she never knew she possessed.

And so, Carissa Moore, the warrior queen of the waves, became Carissa Moore, the warrior queen of juggling. She changed the landscape of professional surfing, showing that motherhood wasn't a sentence to the sidelines, but a ticket to a new kind of power, a success not just for herself, but for every mother who dared to dream of chasing waves and goals without sacrifice. Her story wasn't just about barrels and boards, but about the strong spirit of a woman who made her own path, a mother who rode the waves of life with her children nestled safely in her heart.

Decade of Champions

Consolidating her reputation, World Titles in 2013 and 2014, and becoming a surfing celebrity.

The sun, a melted pearl hanging on the horizon, cast its liquid gold across the quivering painting of the Pacific. Atop it, a figure danced, a melody of balance and grace carved in salty spray. Carissa Moore, in her decade of winners, was painting her legacy on the waves, each flick of her wrist a brushstroke of beauty.

- 13.The year began heavy with the memories of Stephanie Gilmore's successful rule. Yet, Moore, unfazed by the shadow of her rival, made her own way to fame. Bells Beach, Margaret River, Tahiti – each event became a painting where she released her arsenal of power and poise. Her soaring attacks challenged gravity, her rail turns cut lines of craft. Four wins, a choir of cheers, and the crown once again sat upon her head, heavy now, marked with the grit of a hard-fought victory.

- 14. The water, a changeable muse, ordered a new dance. Fiji's Cloudbreak, a whirling beast of a wave, called for fury. Moore, ever the chameleon, adopted the robe of a fighting queen. She controlled the roiling pot, her board a blade slicing through the watery chaos. Bells Beach, once a stage for joy, became a furnace of resilience. A broken fin, a gash on her leg, yet she roared through the pain, her spirit a star in the dying light, taking success from the jaws of loss. Three more jewels added to her crown, each glinting with the fire of her fierce spirit.

But Moore was more than just awards and titles. She was an artist, a creator of feelings on the painting of the wave. Her surfing was a masterpiece made with threads of power and grace, each turn a poem, each barrel dive a whispered secret shared with the ocean. She inspired a generation of girls, her charming smile and fierce drive showing that the ocean accepted not just power, but beauty.

Surfing icon. The name fit her like a well-worn jacket. She graced magazine covers, her name linked with achievement. Yet, she stayed grounded, the girl from Oahu forever marked within the winner. She spoke for the silent, an advocate for the ocean's health, her stage ringing with the roar of the waves she loved.

The decade of winners wasn't just about wins and honors. It was about creating a memory – not in marble or metal, but in the hearts of millions. Carissa Moore, the queen who danced with the wind, the fighter who tamed the storm, the artist who painted with saltwater, had solidified her place in surfing's universe. And as the sun dipped below the horizon, creating long shadows on the water, one thing was certain: her story, like the ocean's tide, would rise again and again, forever etched in the tale of the waves.

PART III

INNOVATION, ADAPTING, AND BEYOND THE COMPETITION (2015-PRESENT)

Beyond the Podium: Carissa Moore's Odyssey of Innovation and Adaptation

When a wave crests at its peak, ready to break, it holds within its twist the potential for both thrilling power and uncertain change. So it was with Carissa Moore, the surfer star who had reached competition heights with a smile and a signature flying style. As the new decade of 2015 opened, her surfboard became a medium for not just winning laps, but a study of unknown surfing areas.

Moore, ever the restless spirit, felt the tug of fresh tasks beyond the organized world tour. The clean barrels of Tahiti called, their green walls demanding a different dance, a deeper connection with the ocean's raw power. Gone were the high-flying moves; instead, she honed her tube-riding skills, contorting her body like a liquid eel within the swirling heart of the wave. Each victorious exit from the barrel's maw was a testament to her daring remake, a win not over rivals, but over the frightening unknown.

But Moore's journey wasn't just about beating foreign waves. It was a journey inwards, a quest to connect with the raw spirit of surfing, stripped bare of competition's stresses. She accepted alternative boards, the enormous noseriders reminiscent of surfing's bygone era, sliding easily across glassy mornings, regaining the joy of simple communication with the water. These were not breaks from her competitive fire, but brushstrokes enriching the weave of her surfing soul.

And yet, the competitive flames still glowed within her. The 2020 Tokyo Olympics loomed, a siren song for any athlete with unfinished Olympic business. Moore, a veteran scarred by the sadness of Athens and the bittersweet success of London, faced Tokyo with the seasoned knowledge of a warrior who knew winning wasn't just about trophies. She rode with the ease of a seasoned narrator, spinning tales of power and accuracy on the waves, eventually winning a bronze that felt like a golden testament to her lasting spirit.

But Moore's influence transcends the boundaries of competition. She became a symbol for ecology, her words matching the ocean's suffering. She championed environmental projects, asking fellow surfers and fans to become protectors of the waves that had given them so much. Her charity, Moore Aloha, fostered the next generation of surfers, encouraging tolerance and a love for the ocean that ran deeper than any prize.

Carissa Moore's story, then, is not just about surfing's energy rush and the golden draw of Olympic success. It's a testament to the human spirit's endless potential for creativity, adaptation, and, above all, connection. It's a lesson that the biggest wins are often not on the platform, but in the quiet moments of daring to ride beyond the known, the familiar, and into the ever-unfurling wave of potential. It's a story that, like the ocean itself, holds within its depths both the thrill of the ride and the wisdom of the beach, saying that the greatest trip is not to the finish line, but to the endless sky of becoming.

Exploring New Frontiers

Experimenting with different boards and techniques, barrel riding, and following big waves.

Carissa Moore, the sun-kissed queen of surfing, carved her name into the sport's history with a fury that reflected the ocean she mastered. But when the cresting waves of competitive power began to smooth, Carissa, ever the restless spirit, refused to be lulled into the doldrums of predictability.

Instead, she went on an exciting journey, a quest for unknown waves and unridden thrills, a testament to her ravenous desire for adventure.

Her surfboard, once a faithful steed in the gladiatorial theater of the World Tour, became a ticket to banned places. She welcomed alternative crafts, the slow grace of longboards telling tales of bygone times, the nimble gymnastics of stand-up paddleboards testing her balance on smooth lakes. In the whirling heart of Tahiti's Teahupoo, she succumbed to the primal appeal of barrel riding, chasing tubes of blue fury, the ocean's green maw threatening to swallow her whole before spitting her out, elated and reborn.

Then came the giants, the leviathans of the deep, their liquid mountains rising from the depths with bone-chilling whispers. Jaws, Mavericks, Nazaré – their names pulsed with danger, a siren song to Carissa's daring soul. She strapped on tow-in boards, rockets powered by energy, and let the jet skis launch her towards nothingness. The world blurred into a collage of spray and fear, the horizon tilted, and then, the wall. A tall giant of water, green and foaming, stood before her, a test of nerve and skill. In that thrilling moment, Carissa was no longer a surfer, but a dancer on the brink of destruction, her board a brushstroke carving defiance on the painting of chaos.

These weren't just adventures; they were pilgrimages, searches for self-discovery amidst the raw woods. Every barrel cut, every giant tamed, chipped away at the mask of the winner, showing the artist, the traveler, the woman beneath the crown. Carissa wasn't just pushing the limits of surfing; she was pushing the boundaries of herself, breaking standards and changing what it meant to be a surfer.

Her journey wasn't always smooth sailing. Wipeouts sent her plummeting through the ocean's vortex, fear eating at her resolve. But Carissa, formed in the furnace of competition, emerged stronger, her spirit a phoenix rising from the foam. Each win, whether over a huge wave or her own self-doubt, rang deeper than any prize.

For Carissa Moore, the boundaries weren't just physical areas; they were psychological settings. Every bold project, every brush with death, revealed a new side of her own resilient spirit. And as she continues to dance on the edge of the unknown, surfboard in hand, heart burning, she tells us that the greatest adventure lies not in defeating waves, but in conquering ourselves.

Advocacy and Environmentalism

Using her platform to raise awareness about ocean protection and sustainability.

Carissa Moore, the queen of surfing, isn't just cutting smooth lines across blue waves. Beneath the sun-kissed skin and salt-streaked hair beats the heart of an ocean fighter, fiercely committed to guarding the playground that made her a hero. Her support for nature isn't some tacked-on addition; it's sewn into the fabric of her being, as natural as the flow of the tide.

Moore's position as a surfing hero echoes like a conch shell across sun-drenched shores. Millions of fans, from grommets getting their first wave to seasoned board experts, hang on her every word. And what she talks of isn't just barrel rolls and perfect 10s, but the quiet language of a threatened ocean.

Her voice, seasoned by the spray of a thousand breaking waves, carries a message of urgency. She speaks of dead coral reefs, the ghosts of lively ecosystems, and the plastic plague choking the lifeblood of the sea. Her words, like breaking waves, break against the apathy of those who turn a blind eye to the ocean's situation.

But Moore isn't just a singer singing about problems. She's a captain, gathering a group of changemakers. Her foundation, Moore Aloha Ohana, encourages young surfers to become ocean guardians, teaching them the delicate dance between riding waves and respecting their watery home. Educational programs, beach cleanups, and sustainable projects – these are the tools in her collection, handled with the ease of a backside 360 and the drive of a paddling into a ten-foot wall of water.

Her campaigning isn't confined to dry land or slick talks. Moore walks the walk, her board a pulpit from which she teaches by example. She promotes sustainable surfwear, works with eco-conscious brands, and even creates her own line of ocean-friendly goods. Every wave she catches, every move she performs, becomes a quiet ode to the health of the seas.

And it's not just about saving turtles and coral reefs. Moore knows the complex web that binds the ocean to humans. She supports clean water projects, knowing that healthy waves mean healthy communities. She talks of climate change, the unseen wave threatening seaside havens, and begs for action before the tide of inaction swallows us whole.

Carissa Moore isn't just a surfer. She's a force of nature, a wave of change crashing against the beaches of apathy. Her voice, boosted by her ability and platform, rings out across the world, asking us to listen to the ocean's words before its roar becomes a thundering cry. Because in the end, saving the waves that made her a winner is not just about preserving a sport, it's about preserving the very breath of life itself. And that, dear reader, is a wave worth riding.

Mentoring the Next Generation

Inspiring young surfers, guiding camps, and building a welcoming community.

Carissa Moore, the sun-kissed queen of surfing, wasn't happy simply ruling the waves. Her desire, like the wave, went further, pulling a generation of young riders in its wake. Mentoring became her second wave, cresting with a force as strong as her signature aerials.

Coaching camps grew under her golden touch, not on boring asphalt tracks, but on the vast painting of the ocean. Picture sun-drenched beaches ringing with the shrieks of laughter as grommets, the surfing world's term for kids, paddled out under Carissa's watchful eye. No drill master barking orders here, just the gentle melody of praise and helpful feedback, each word as uplifting as a perfectly timed bottom turn.

Carissa understood the language of young surfers, the hidden fears that lurked beneath the confidence. She'd been there, a skinny youth with saltwater running through her blood and dreams as vast as the Pacific. Her words, seasoned with the knowledge of countless wipeouts and wins, reverberated, banishing fear and sparking confidence.

But Carissa's guidance wasn't just about professional ability. It was about building out a community, a safe port where frailty wasn't weakness, but the rich ground for growth. She championed girls' surfing, her own journey a testament to the power of overcoming norms. She built bonds across groups, her infectious smile removing cultural differences as easily as she floated across smooth waves.

Think of her as a guide in the rough seas of youth. Her every action, from sharing tips on cutting lines to planning beach cleanups, served as a light, leading young surfers towards not just surfing greatness, but a life of purpose and environmental care.

One could see her impact marked on the sun-bronzed faces of her mentees, not just in their honed skills, but in their steadfast support for each other. Carissa had spun a web of friendship, a clan formed in the furnace of shared love and respect for the ocean's fickle embrace.

So, the next time you watch a young surfer cutting impossible lines, remember the woman who helped them find their balance, not just on the board, but in the face of life's inevitable swells. Carissa Moore, the winner, the guide, the queen who made a wave of hope, one grommet at a time.

The Tokyo Games and Beyond

Competing in the 2020 Olympics, adjusting to changed surf styles, and meeting new difficulties.

The sun beat down on Tsurigasaki Beach, its merciless eyes changing the sand to molten gold. The Pacific, usually a playful child, lay flat and blue, holding its breath for the coming drama. For Carissa Moore, it was a familiar set, yet one that had undergone a slight transformation. Tokyo 2020 was not just another Olympics; it was a Rubicon, splitting the known beaches of her control from the unfamiliar seas of a changed sport.

The years since Rio had been a lesson in adaptation. The younger guard, driven by daring flying moves and lightning-fast turns, were nipping at her heels. Gone were the days of brute power defining success; subtlety and creativity were the new currency. Moore, the clear queen of strong calves and bottom turns, knew she had to change.

She accepted the transformation like a lizard losing its skin. Hours were spent analyzing videos of her younger foes, carefully deconstructing their flying ballets. Her board, once a trusty horse, was changed for a lighter, more flexible craft, eager to soar. The salt-kissed spray that once stung her eyes now held the promise of new options.

Tokyo was her testing ground. The world watched with bated breath as she launched a range of previously unknown moves. There were high airs defying gravity, daring spins copying flying ballerinas, and audacious barrel rides that played with the lip of nothingness. It was a song of power and ease, a lesson in transformation.

But the road wasn't lined with sun-kissed waves and perfect moves. Frustration gnawed at her when gravity failed her flying goals, when boards were snapped by harsh lips, and when younger surfers danced through the water with an easy beat that seemed to escape her. Doubt, that cunning snake, began to coil around her heart.

Yet, Moore, the phoenix of surfing, had risen from the ashes of disappointment too many times to be daunted. She dug deep, her competitive fire refusing to be extinguished. She sought comfort in the familiar beat of the ocean, the language of waves a balm to her soul. In the quiet connection with the sea, she found the joy of pure surfing, the uninhibited thrill of riding the edge of chaos.

And so, on that fateful day in Tokyo, under the burning sun, she found her salvation. Not in a golden prize, though that would have been a sweet conclusion, but in a performance that transcended mere competition. It was a lesson in perseverance, a testament to the resilient spirit of a winner who refused to be defined by age or style.

Carissa Moore stood on the platform, the silver award a sign of pride, not failure. The years to come, she knew, held new trials, new waves to beat. But as she gazed at the ocean, a playful glint in her eyes, one thing was certain: Carissa Moore, the ageless surfer, was just getting started. The Tokyo Games were not a conclusion, but an exciting new chapter in the tale of the surfer queen.

Life Beyond the Competition

Philanthropy, business, and finding balance in a post-competitive job.

Carving New Waves: Carissa Moore's Life Beyond the Podium
Like a tired wave retreating from the shore, Carissa Moore's professional career ebbed with grace. But unlike the ocean's quiet retreat, her exit from the title tour resonated with the wave of a thousand new starts. It was a transformation more subtle than a barrel roll, yet just as changing, as the queen of surfing traded polluted victory laps for the open waters of charity, business, and a life richly colored with shades beyond gold medals.

Moore's philanthropic spirit, ever present during her rule, bloomed with greater freedom. Her foundation, Moore Aloha Ohana, grew into a lively coral reef of community projects. From funding surf camps for poor youth to leading ocean protection projects, she nurtured the very waves that had carried her to greatness. Her infectious excitement not only enabled impoverished kids but also inspired fellow surfers, creating a patchwork of environmental action as vast and linked as the Pacific itself.

But Moore's goal wasn't to merely tread water. The business fire that had always flickered beneath the sun-kissed skin of the winner sparked. Carissa Moore Eco, a sustainable swimwear line made from recycled ocean plastics, appeared as a testament to her commitment to both style and the environment. It was a deliberate revolt against the fast-fashion tide, a wave of eco-friendly bikinis and boardshorts smashing onto the beaches of conscious shopping.

Yet, amidst the whirl of giving back and building businesses, Moore's most meaningful journey unfolded inwards. Stepping off the competition treadmill allowed her to reunite with the simple joys of riding waves for the sheer love of it. No longer chasing points or standings, she explored new parts of her sport, chasing rare barrels in Tahiti and cutting lines down epic Indonesian walls. In this rediscovery of pure surfing pleasure, she rediscovered herself, showing that sometimes the best prizes are found not on podiums, but in the quiet connection with the ocean and the words of one's own soul.

This wasn't an escape into quietude, however. Moore accepted the role of guide, her knowledge honed in the fire of competition now leading a new generation of surfers. Through camps, workshops, and internet lessons, she poured her knowledge back into the sport that had given her so much. In the eyes of wide-eyed grommets hanging onto her every word, she saw not just future winners, but caretakers of the ocean, torchbearers of the environmental armor she had so fiercely thrown over surfing's shoulders.

Carissa Moore's life beyond the race is a testament to the varied nature of a winner. It's a colorful fabric made with strings of giving back, building a sustainable future, and regaining the joy of pure surfing. It's a lesson that success comes in many ways, not just on scoreboards, but in the quiet waves of good change that one life can make. And as she carves new waves in this unknown chapter, one thing stays certain: Carissa Moore, the queen of surfing, is far from done making waves.

CONCLUSION

Carissa's Legacy:

Carissa Moore: Where Ocean and Aloha Collide
Born on Oahu's sun-kissed shores, Carissa Moore wasn't just cradled by the Pacific. She was woven into its beat, bathed in its salt, and molded by its endless power. The water wasn't just her playroom; it was her heritage, her palette, her soul's guide. And on that canvas, she hasn't painted mere splashes; she's created a heritage as bright as a Hawaiian sunset.

Her tale starts not with awards, but with bare feet walking across coral-strewn sand, a four-year-old drawn to the ocean's pulse like a baby seabird to the horizon. Her surfboard, soon an extension of her own limbs, became a chariot to dance on green waves, cutting lines of liquid poetry with the ease of a moana (ocean queen).

Teenage fame wasn't a flash; it was a managed burn. At 18, she became the youngest surfer, male or female, to win the World Title, her ability an explosion that sent shockwaves through the sport. But Carissa never mistook praise for purpose. Her smile, as brilliant as a plumeria bloom, held the quiet knowledge of the ancient Hawaiians, the "aloha spirit" woven into her every move.

She conquered waves with the fury of a tiger shark, yet floated through them with the grace of a manta ray. Her surfing wasn't just a dance of gymnastics; it was a connection with the water, a quiet conversation of respect and awe. Carissa wasn't just catching waves; she was speaking their language, turning their words into stunning shows.

Her impact, however, surpasses the white foam. It's not just etched in medals or etched in digital Olympic gold, but weaved into the minds of the next generation. Through her organization, Moore Aloha, she fosters the dreams of young girls, telling them that the ocean calls not just with waves, but with endless possibilities.

Carissa Moore isn't just a surfer; she's a force of nature, a live expression of Hawaiian energy. And as she carves her way through the ever-changing waves of life, one thing stays constant: the deep connection between her soul and the ocean, a memory that will continue to ripple long after the last wave breaks.

So, when you see Carissa Moore sliding across the liquid blue, remember, you're not just witnessing sports ability; you're witnessing a melody of ocean and spirit, a heritage echoing on the shores of time, speaking the timeless beauty of a life lived in perfect balance with the waves.

Impact on surfing: Revolutionizing women's surfing, raising the bar of achievement, and inspiring a generation.

Carissa Moore wasn't just a wave-taming wonder; she was a storm that changed the world of women's surfing. Before Carissa paddled out, the women's competition scene was a sun-kissed picture – fluid moves, modest smiles, and scores that hung nicely in the single digits. Then came Carissa, a storm in a bikini, her board an extension of her will, cutting impossible lines into the face of the wave with bold power and audacious style.

She didn't just win; she changed. Her aerial attacks – the daring airs, the gravity-defying spins – made jaws drop and scores explode. She wasn't just riding the wave; she was owning it, her body a blur of controlled anger against the painting of the ocean. The judges, used to tiny dabs and polite turns, rushed to find words to describe the storm they were watching. "Radical," "audacious," "groundbreaking" – even those felt like understatements in the face of Carissa's attack.

But Carissa's effect wasn't just about pushing the edge of technique. It was about breaking the glass roof of standards. When Carissa surfed, she didn't surf like a girl; she surfed like a force of nature, as strong and wild as the ocean itself. This wasn't a delicate ballet; it was a wild dance with the elements, a bold show of raw power and speed that changed what it meant to be a female surfer.

And the little girls on the beach, watching Carissa paint the waves with her anger, took notice. They saw not just a winner, but a mirror of their own limitless promise. They saw that surfing wasn't just about looking good; it was about pushing limits, breaking standards, and making your own path. Carissa wasn't just winning events; she was winning hearts, inspiring a generation of girls to grab their boards and change the story of women's surfing.

The waves of Carissa's impact went beyond the competition field. She became a sign of women's strength, her every aerial attack a defiant middle finger to outdated ideas of femininity. She made magazine covers, became a brand spokeswoman, and used her position to fight for environmental issues and ocean protection. Carissa wasn't just a surfer; she was a role model, a changemaker, a living testament to the power of one woman to rewrite the rules and inspire a generation to chase their own impossible waves.

So, when we talk about Carissa Moore's effect, we don't just talk about prizes and points. We talk about a seismic change in the very DNA of women's surfing. We talk about a group of girls who dared to dream big, who saw the ocean not as a playground for boys, but as their own personal painting, ready to be painted with their own wild rage. We talk about Carissa Moore, the wave-taming wonder who wasn't just a winner; she was a change.

Beyond the sport: Role model for sports and women, supporting ecology, and making a long mark.

Carissa Moore is a wave whisperer, a queen of her watery realm, but her rule stretches far beyond the frothy country of competition surfing. She's a force of nature who sculpts not just loops and turns, but a future built on equality, environmentalism, and the unshakeable belief that anything, even riding a ten-foot wall of water, is within reach.

As a role model for sports, she's not just a prize collector, but a master class in endurance. Remember the painful near-miss of Athens 2004?

The sadness that could have eaten her whole? Instead, she used it as fuel, her drive hardening like sunbaked coral, driving her to Olympic gold in London eight years later. She teaches young surfers, girls and boys alike, that failures are not stop signs, but detours on the road to greatness.

Beyond the field, Carissa promotes women in a sport once ruled by bronzed, sun-bleached guys. She speaks in boardrooms and seaside bonfires, her voice a trumpet for gender equality, breaking stereotypes like driftwood on a rough shore. She's not just riding waves, she's riding the tide of change, showing that power and grace can live in a salty spray of rebellion.

Her environmental action isn't some PR-polished surface, it's woven into the fabric of her being. She's a representative for the fragile ocean, its coral towers and whispered whales her kin. She created the Moore Aloha Foundation, a light of hope for saving the very playground that made her a hero. In her, the spirit of old Hawaiian defenders dances, telling us that respecting the ocean isn't choice, it's a heritage.

Carissa Moore's impact won't be measured in medals or world titles, though her cabinet moans under their weight. It will be etched in the hearts of young girls who dared to dream of making their own tracks on liquid slopes. It will be mentioned in the swaying palm trees, a testament to the woman who fought for a better, kinder ocean. It will be the sound of her laughter, the spray of her board cutting through the waves, a steady reminder that even the most epic trips begin with a single, brave run.

So, when you see Carissa Moore, don't just see a surfing star. See a creator of ideas, a fighter for the blue planet, and a testament to the lasting power of the human spirit. She's not just riding waves, she's riding the top of a movement, leaving behind a wake of energy that will take us all, surfers and landlubbers alike, to a brighter, more hopeful beach.

Thanks you for your Purchase!

You can help us by dropping an honest rating and review.

Going to mean a lot to us

Printed in Great Britain
by Amazon